To Eric,

Silva '06

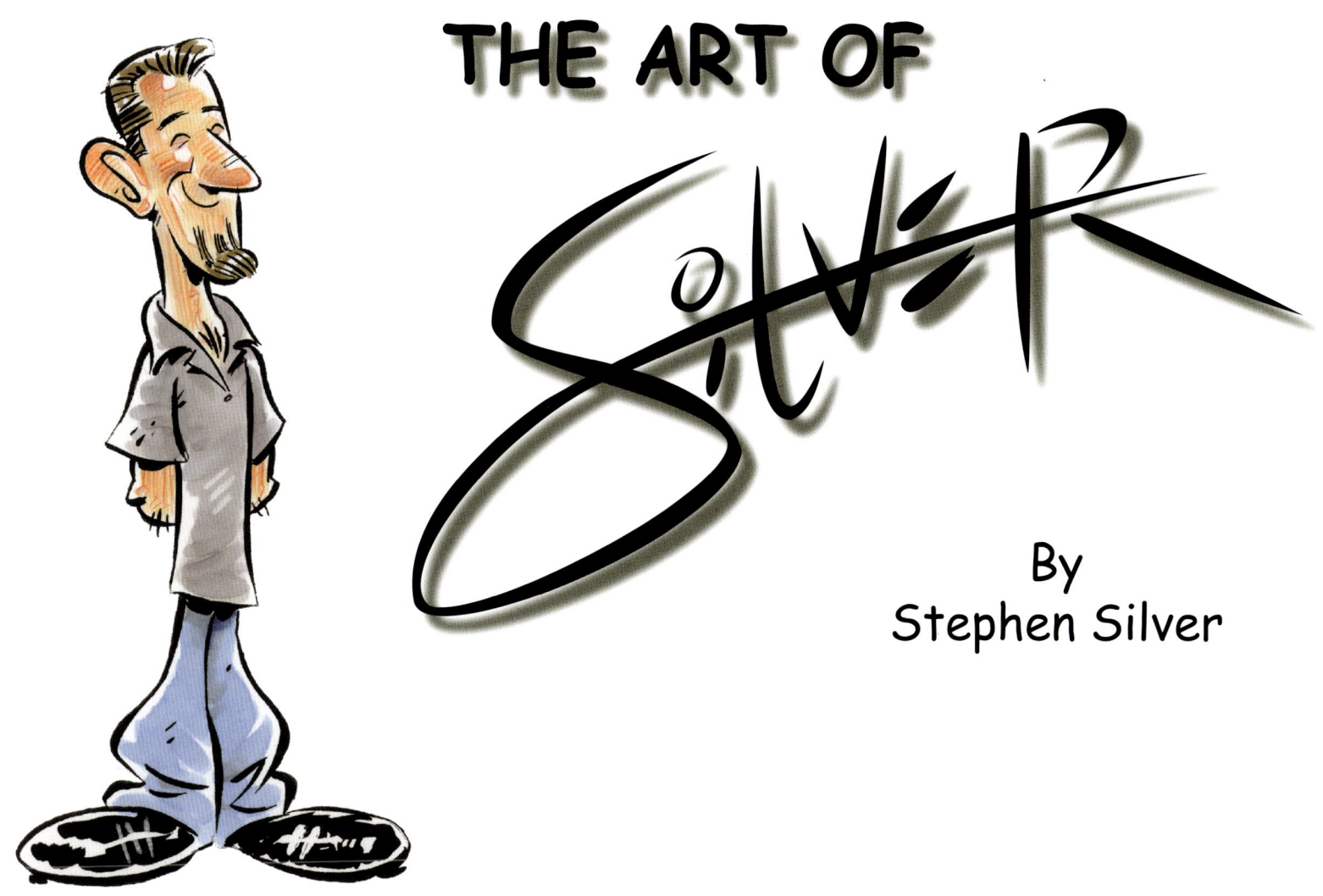

THE ART OF Silver

By
Stephen Silver

Foreword by Kevin Smith
Additional words by: Jack Davis and Tom Richmond

The Art of Silver, by Stephen Silver
Copyright © 2004 by Stephen Silver/Silvertoons
Used by permission. Clerks and all characters TM & ©2004 View Askew Productions, Inc. All Rights Reserved. Kevin Smith, Used by permission.©2004 Viacom International Inc. All Rights Reserved. Nickelodeon, The Fairly OddParents and all related titles, logos and characters are trademarks of Viacom International Inc. All artwork in this book, unless otherwise attributed are copyright ©2004 Stephen Silver. Any similarity, without satiric purpose, to any person, living or dead, portrayed or depicted in this book is purely coincidental.

All rights reserved. No part of this book may be reproduced or used in any format or in any medium without the written permission of the publisher

Published by Silvertoons
263 Rustling Heights Ct. Suite 172
Simi Valley, CA 93065

Book designed by Stephen Silver

Library of Congress Control Number: 2003096758

ISBN 0-9745701-0-9 (Hardcover Vol.1)

Printed in China

Second Printing

10 9 8 7 6 5 4 3 2

Visit Stephen Silver on the web at
www.silvertoons.com

This book is dedicated to my family, Heidi, Caiden and Macey and to all the artists that have inspired me throughout my life.

ACKNOWLEDGMENTS

I would like to thank my wife, Heidi, for her tremendous enthusiasm, support and understanding of my art. She has made it possible for me to live a normal balanced life and gets me out of the house from time to time.
I would like to give special thanks to my friend Steve Fishwick for his help in scanning the many images and encouraging me to make this book. Michel Gagne for all his helpful information into self publishing. Mark Taylor at Nickelodeon for his help and support. Ben and Becca Balistreri, Frank Rocco, Avalon-Chava Pelleg, Paul Silver and Cynthia True for their superb editing skills. I would also like to thank Kevin Smith, Jack Davis, Mort Drucker, John Kascht, Butch Hartman and Tom Richmond for their beautifully written contributions to this book. Last but not least a big thanks to my parents for bringing me into this world and supporting my art from early on.

-- Stephen Silver

Foreword

Of the many things I can't do very well, drawing tops the list. If you ask me to illustrate a cat, you'll get back a piece of paper worn through with erasure marks, between which lies an unsettling clump of roundish lines that vaguely resemble *some* form of quadraped, dotted with pointy ears and monstrously disproportionate tail and whiskers. Hang it up in a pre-school classroom, and it'd invoke not only sympathy, but also speculation that it was the sketch of a four year old who was raised in a Skinner Box, with only the *description* of a cat to go by for his first attempt at basic-level communication.

For this and many other reasons, I have the utmost respect for people who *can* draw… and flat-out *awe* for people who can draw insanely *well*.

Like my friend Stephen Silver.

I met Stephen while working on the ill-fated, short-lived "Clerks" cartoon back in 2000. He was a character design guy, hand-picked by our director Chris Bailey to flesh out and populate our animated world. When given the task of creating a look for Mister Plug (the henchman/publicist of our villain/Mr. Burns-rip-off Leonardo Leonardo), Stephen turned in a spot-on likeness of OddJob from the Connery Bond film "Goldfinger". It was an image that immediately invoked the source, *and* made you chuckle – the mark of good satirical cartooning.

When the show went in the shitter, I'd call Stephen from time to time to draw things for my production company, View Askew. Whether it was a new character design for a t-shirt or a simple logo for a mini-film fest, Stephen was always able to visually realize my ideas for me, and bring a little something special to the table in the process. It's one thing to provide an artist with the basic direction "Silent Bob should be eating popcorn." It's quite another thing when the artist presents you with a mid-chew, puffy cheeked, cartoon version of yourself that's so strikingly original, it makes you giggle as if you'd never asked for the drawing in the first place.

When we decided to start making a line of InAction figures based on the characters in our five film View Askewniverse, Stephen was brought on to render what the sculptor would later turn into 3D versions of his drawings. When I wanted to create a new logo for my production company that featured the characters I just can't escape (Jay and Silent Bob), I gave Stephen a brief description of what I was looking for, and he turned in genius. I can't relate the simple joy in knowing a go-to guy who can bring your thoughts to life; a gifted guy who can *be* your hands.

However, as you'll see in the following pages, Stephen's far more than just a guy who draws my dopey nonsense. His character studies run the gamut from cartoony to poetic; from belly-laughs to beautiful. You're holding a small sampling of the work of a true artist – a true artist who, thankfully, slums it with the likes of me and mine, from time to time. And my world is all the better for his charitable low standards.

So if you're looking for someone to draw you a cat, gimme a shout. I'll put you in touch with a guy who can do that and so much more.

Ladies and gentlemen, I give you Stephen Silver.

Kevin Smith

A very special foreword that Jack Davis sent to me especially for this book.

INTRODUCTION

I was born in London, England in 1972 and am one of five children, including my twin brother Graham. In 1981, at the age of nine, my family moved to San Diego, California. I lived there until moving to Los Angeles in 1997. I have always loved to draw. At the age of six, I found an artist's sketchbook lying in my backyard. I picked it up and carried it everywhere I went. From that moment on, I have never stopped drawing.

I was never a good student in school. I received poor grades in all of my classes, including art. In high school, I drew cartoons for the school newspaper (as well as on all of my homework). At the age of 17, on a family vacation to Las Vegas, I found a direction for what I wanted to do with my life. Instead of hanging out with my parents, I spent my time watching caricature artists draw in the casino we were staying in. The manager of the caricature concession stand noticed my fascination. He told me to practice drawing caricatures and submit my work to him if I wanted a job. When I got home, I drew every famous person I could think of, as well as half of the people in my high school yearbook. When I was 18 years old, I heard that Sea World was looking for caricaturists. I showed up for my interview with long hair, an earring, slippers with duct tape around them and a torn plastic bag containing my artwork. They seemed desperate for an artist and hired me on the spot. I did, however, have to lose the earring and the mullet. During the first week at Sea World, I was offered the job in Las Vegas. I politely declined and decided to stay in San Diego.

After my second semester of Junior College, I quit in order to work full time at Sea World. I could no longer focus in school and I knew that if I wanted to be a successful artist I would need a good portfolio, not grades. My parents always encouraged my art, but had no idea what I should do with it. They would give me the typical line: "Go to college, get good grades and then you will be successful." They weren't thrilled with my decision to stop going to school and told me if I dropped out I would have to financially support myself on every level. It was the best thing they could have done for me. It gave me the drive and motivation to succeed in the art field.

Jack Davis's studio August 2003

At that point in my life, I was very fortunate to have a mentor, David Kamish, who was an inspiration to me. He was responsible for hiring me and pushed me to develop my skills as a caricaturist and encouraged me to draw constantly. He taught me that there are no rules in art. You can draw whatever you want. Soon my observation skills improved as well as my confidence and speed. My friendship with David provided another important lesson: learn from other artists that inspire you. He introduced me to the work of artists who drew for Mad Magazine, Mort Drucker and Jack Davis. Through their great work, they would become my motivation, and my mentors. I learned from Mort to get a better understanding of structure and form. When I had the pleasure of meeting him at the San Diego Comic Convention in 1996 he reminded me that, with art, there is no magic, that everything takes time and practice. Jack Davis's work taught me to stay loose, animate and create energy within a drawing. When I had the pleasure of meeting Jack in his studio in Georgia, he expressed to me those same ideas and told me to have fun and make people smile.

In the winter of 1992 I ended up in Minnesota, where I worked in the Mall of America. I drew caricatures almost seven days a week. On my day off, I happened to stumble upon Tom Richmond (who is now prominently featured in Mad Magazine) drawing in another mall. I was so amazed by his skill, that watching him draw became a second job for me. I finally summoned the courage to speak to him, and within the next couple of days he offered me a summer job working for him at Valley Fair Amusement Park in Minnesota. I spent more time watching him draw that summer than I did drawing.

Upon returning home, I set up my own business called Silvertoons. The business mainly consisted of drawing caricatures at events and cartoon commissions. I also set up caricature concession stands in shopping malls during Christmas for the next three years, and had a concession stand at the Barona Casino in San Diego.

During Christmas of 1996, as I was drawing caricatures at the mall, the art team from the clothing company *No Fear* approached me. They asked if I would like to work for them when Christmas was over. So, in January of 1997, I showed up with my drawings at their office in Carlsbad, California and was hired.

That year my parents gave me a newspaper article about the animation boom. I decided to submit my work to Warner Bros. Animation Studios. I made some copies from my sketchbooks, put in some life drawings, made my own portfolio case out of wood and drove to Los Angeles to drop off my work. It was at that point that my art career took a different direction. I had an opportunity to take a character design test for the show "Histeria." It was caricature heavy, my specialty. My assignment was to design three historical characters of my choice and I was told to bring them back the following week. I went home that night drew King Henry the VIII, Al Capone and Adolf Hitler and showed up at the studio two days later with an armful of drawings. When I am given a test, I tend to go overboard drawing pages of designs, even if they only require a few. My approach is to be fast, efficient and on time. I distinctly remember sitting with my friend, Steve Fishwick, and getting a phone call from Warner Bros. offering me the job. Not only was I speechless, but I remember them asking, "So, aren't you going to ask how much you're going to make?" Frankly, I didn't care. I was about to embark on another great journey. I was about to become a Warner Bros. animation artist!

It was Bob Doucette, director of "Histeria," who was responsible for giving me my big break. Bob took me under his wing. It is very rare to find a director who will take the time, as Bob did, to teach me the tools of the trade. I started taking some nightly character design and life drawing classes. I couldn't get enough. When "Histeria" ended I went on to art direct a show that Bob had created called "Detention."

In August of 1999, I left Warner Bros. to work for Disney Television Animation on "Clerks: The Animated Series." I had the opportunity to take a test designing the main characters; Dante, Randal, Jay and Mr. Plug (Silent Bob had already been designed). After several meetings with the show's director, Chris Bailey, I was hired. Chris was once a Disney feature animator and is an amazing artist. The opportunity to work with him on a day-to-day basis developing the characters was a great learning experience. Unfortunately, the series was cancelled after airing only two episodes out of the six that were produced. The show, however, connected me with the creator, Kevin Smith. He put out the whole series on DVD and later I was contacted by him to design the "Clerks" Inaction Figure toy line. In 2000, I received a call from Chris about developing the characters for a brand new show at Disney called "Kim Possible." For this show, I turned to another of my artistic influences, world famous caricaturist, Al Hirschfeld. I have always been moved by his rhythmical line and tried to bring that sensibility to "Kim Possible."

In November 2001, after the first season of "Kim Possible," I received a call from Bob Boyle, the Art Director for Nickelodeon's "The Fairly OddParents." They were in the process of developing a brand new show called "Danny Phantom," created by "The Fairly OddParents" creator, Butch Hartman. I dropped off my portfolio and within a few days got the call to come in to meet Butch and take a test. Butch is truly one of a kind, a man who has achieved a great deal and can do it all. From writing, directing and storyboarding to timing, animating, designing, song writing and voice acting. So, it was a great honor to work with him on a new project from the ground-up. During a break in the "Phantom" development schedule, I had the opportunity to work side by side with a great designer, Ben Balistreri, a longtime Disney artist. We were given the opportunity to develop another Butch Hartman/Steve Marmel production, " Crash Nebula." We based the show's look on the work of some great French comic artists like Uderzo, Leturgie, and Conrad. It was an enjoyable experience, once again, to create the look of a project from the beginning.

Outside of work, I was developing my own animated TV series and comic book called "Wildlife Force™." Also during this time, I published a thirty-two page sketchbook in black and white comic book format. Due to the overwhelming response of the sketchbook, I felt it was time for me to take the next step and create this new hardcover version.

As an artist, I continue to search for new ways to draw. Uninhibited by style or rules, I am constantly motivated to improve my craft. It is exciting for me to look back at my sketchbooks from year to year and see how my artwork is developing. I believe that what Mort Drucker said is true: "There is no magic in art." The dedication and desire that I have as an artist will help me reach high artistic goals.

I believe the success I have achieved as an artist can be attributed to my ability to draw in many different styles. In the animation industry, versatility is an asset. Committing myself to becoming a full-time artist at a young age was the best decision I ever made. As long as I keep drawing, I know I'll keep improving. Drawing has become an addiction for me, a habit I cannot break. I feed my addiction by drawing in my sketchbook every single day. It feels great!

Within this book, I present a collection of drawings from my sketchbooks, various caricatures, character designs and some illustration work. Most of the drawings in this book are figments of my imagination, others are drawn from observation and photos. It is my hope that this book inspires you like so many other artists have inspired me. Enjoy!

Helpful Drawing Tips

1) Always carry a sketchbook. Observe real life and draw from books and magazines with good photos.

2) Learn from other artists. I heard a saying once: "Mimicry is the prerequisite to creativity." If there are artists you admire, practice drawing the way they do and try to learn what they have learned.

3) Take some life drawing classes, but don't just copy the model - make them skinnier or fatter, using different mediums every time you draw.

4) Learn to draw caricatures. It will help you with exaggeration and improve your designs in the long run. Get a job drawing live caricatures. It will build up your speed and confidence in drawing as well as your observation skills.

5) Surround yourself with other artists. Learn from them or just go and draw with them. It will motivate you to draw more.

6) Become a member of a cartoonist organization, such as the National Caricaturist Network or your local Cartoonists Society. You will get a chance to meet some very talented people and, once again, it will inspire you to draw more.

7) Never believe that you are good enough. There is always room for improvement.

8) Be patient. You will need it as there is no magic and it will not happen overnight. It takes time. Have the desire to be the best artist you can be and have the determination to achieve whatever it is you wish to do with your art career.

9) Don't be afraid to fail and ***HAVE FUN!***

10) Did I mention...always carry a sketchbook!!!

"Excellence is never granted to man but as the reward of labor."--- Sir Joshua Reynolds.

Above: This is one of the earliest drawings I could find. I was 13 years old at the time.

> **WARNING:**
> The drawings featured on these pages were drawn over 12 years ago. I felt it was necessary to include these pages to show you the level I was at right after high school. So if you are young or old, don't be discouraged. Drawing takes practice and patience and most of all, time.

As you can see, there are no confident lines.

Some early caricature work. No sense of construction.

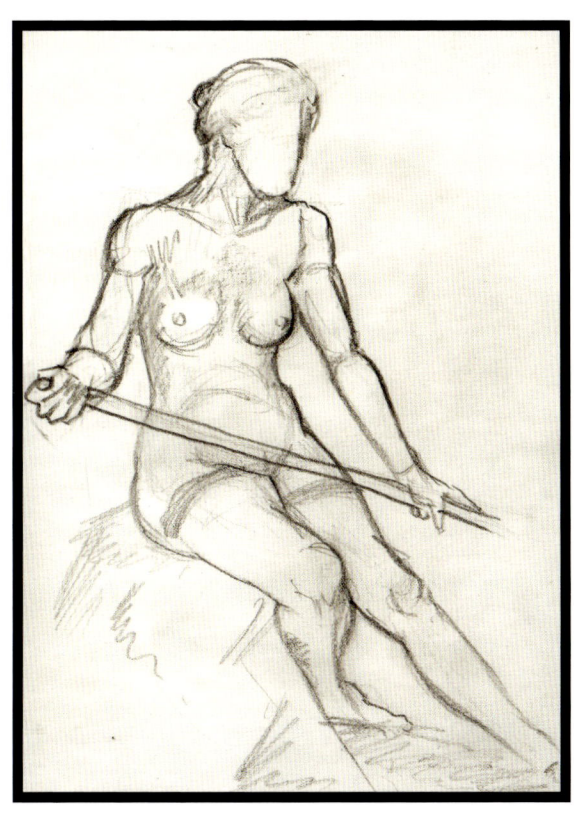

It is amusing to me as I re-look at these and remember, how at that time, I was proud of myself.

These life drawings were done at my first and only year of Jr. College. I was 18 years old at the time and had no understanding of anatomy or construction. But, I was always determined to get better and later enrolled in some life drawing classes.

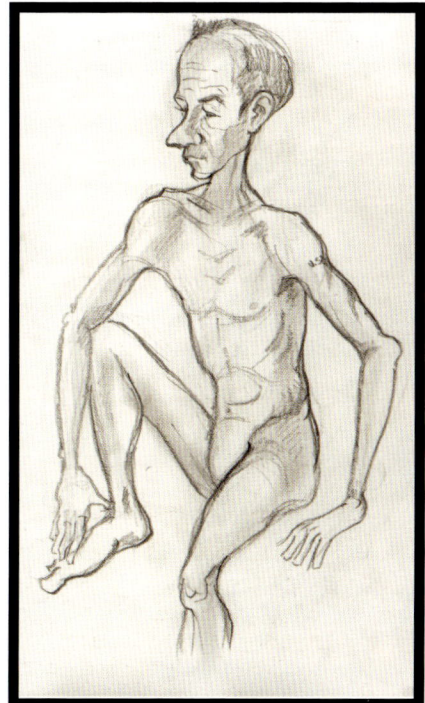

This figure was drawn from a live model using colored pencils.

The drawings on the opposite page and following two pages were done on leftover scraps of 100 lb. Bristol board that were about to be thrown away. Once I saw the strips of paper, I got inspired and it led to these random heads that are drawn in marker and colored pencil. The slightest thing can inspire a new idea for me and that's what makes art so much fun.

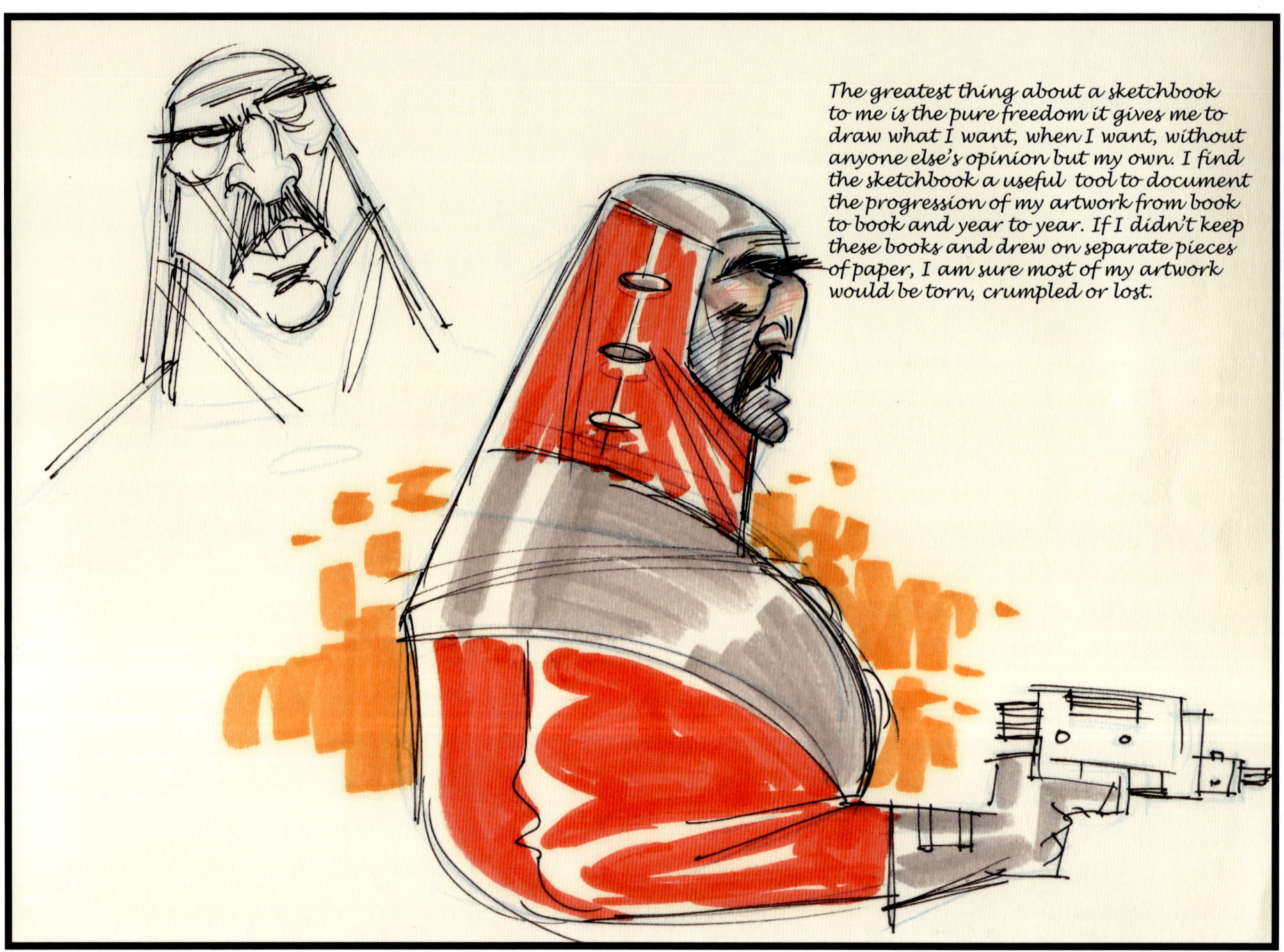

Below: Charcoal and Prismacolor pencil.

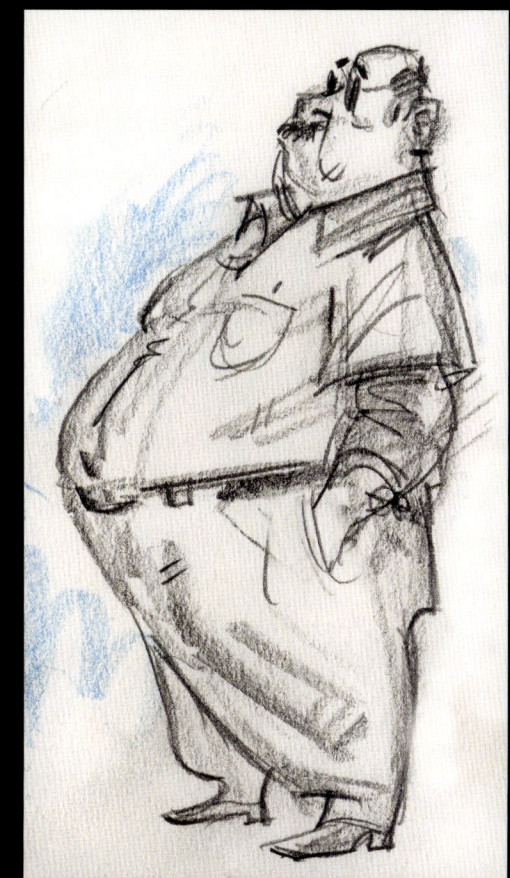

As you can see, my favorite things to draw are heads. To me they are the most intriguing part of a person. I look at them all day long and there is so much personality and expression. These were drawn using a Pilot Razor Point pen.

I collect many books with old black and white movie stills in them. They are a great source of reference for character types, fashion and poses. When I am not drawing from life or out of my head, I will pick out one of these books and start drawing.

If you are still reading at this point, I am about to disclose one of my biggest drawing techniques. Most of the designs I draw, I start with the figure eight. The picture above demonstrates this technique. All I did was squash and stretch the number and before I knew it, I had an instant variety within my shapes.

These were drawn with blue pencil and then loosely inked with a Fountain Pentel. I often don't know what I am going to draw until my pen or pencil hits the paper. However, the times I do make a commitment and know what it is I want to draw, I tend to have more success. Hence the term I like to use "What's the story?"

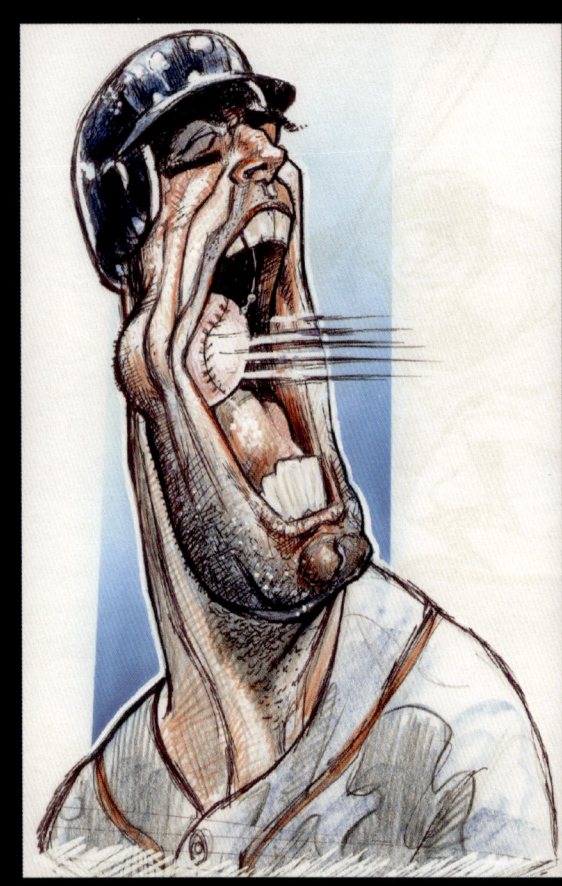

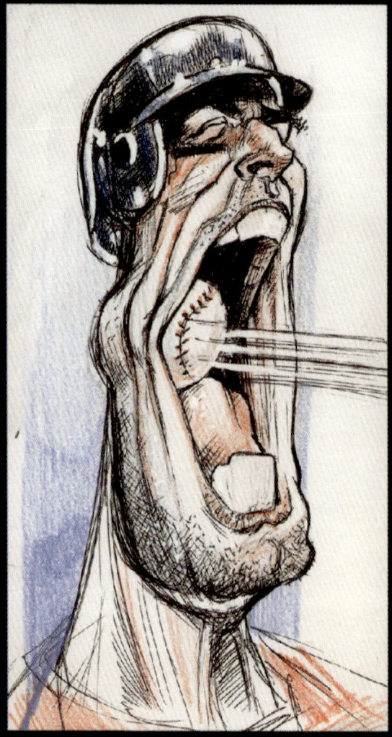

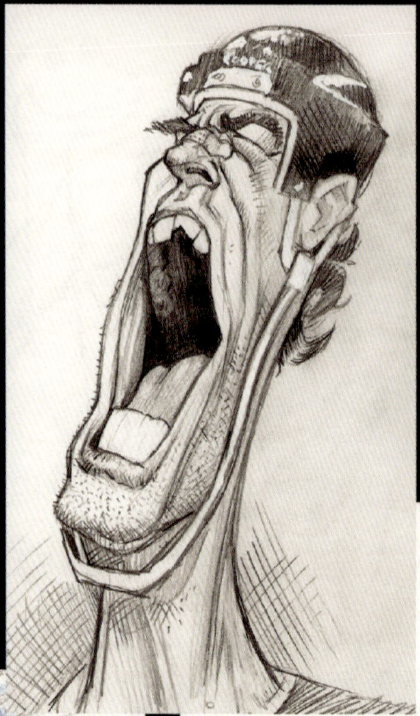

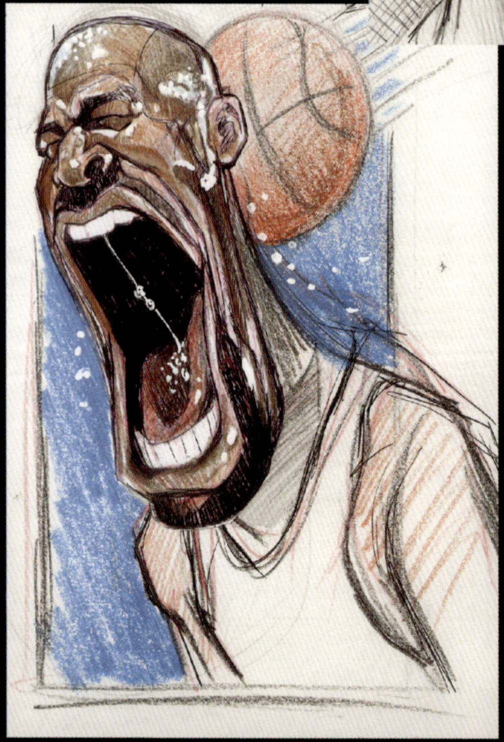

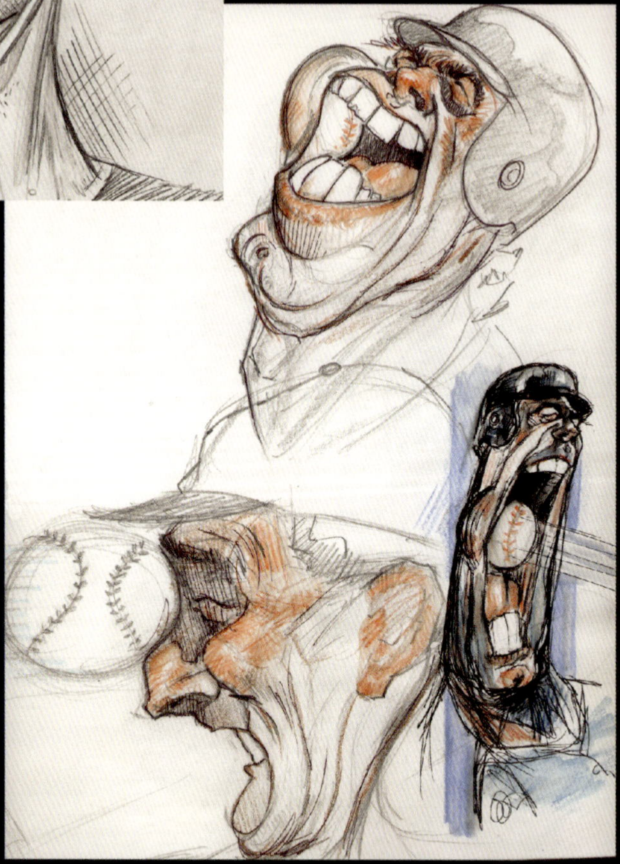

Preliminary sketches for the opposite drawings. I used HB/B pencils, felt tip pens and colored pencils.

Opposite:
The final pieces completed in airbrush and colored pencil.

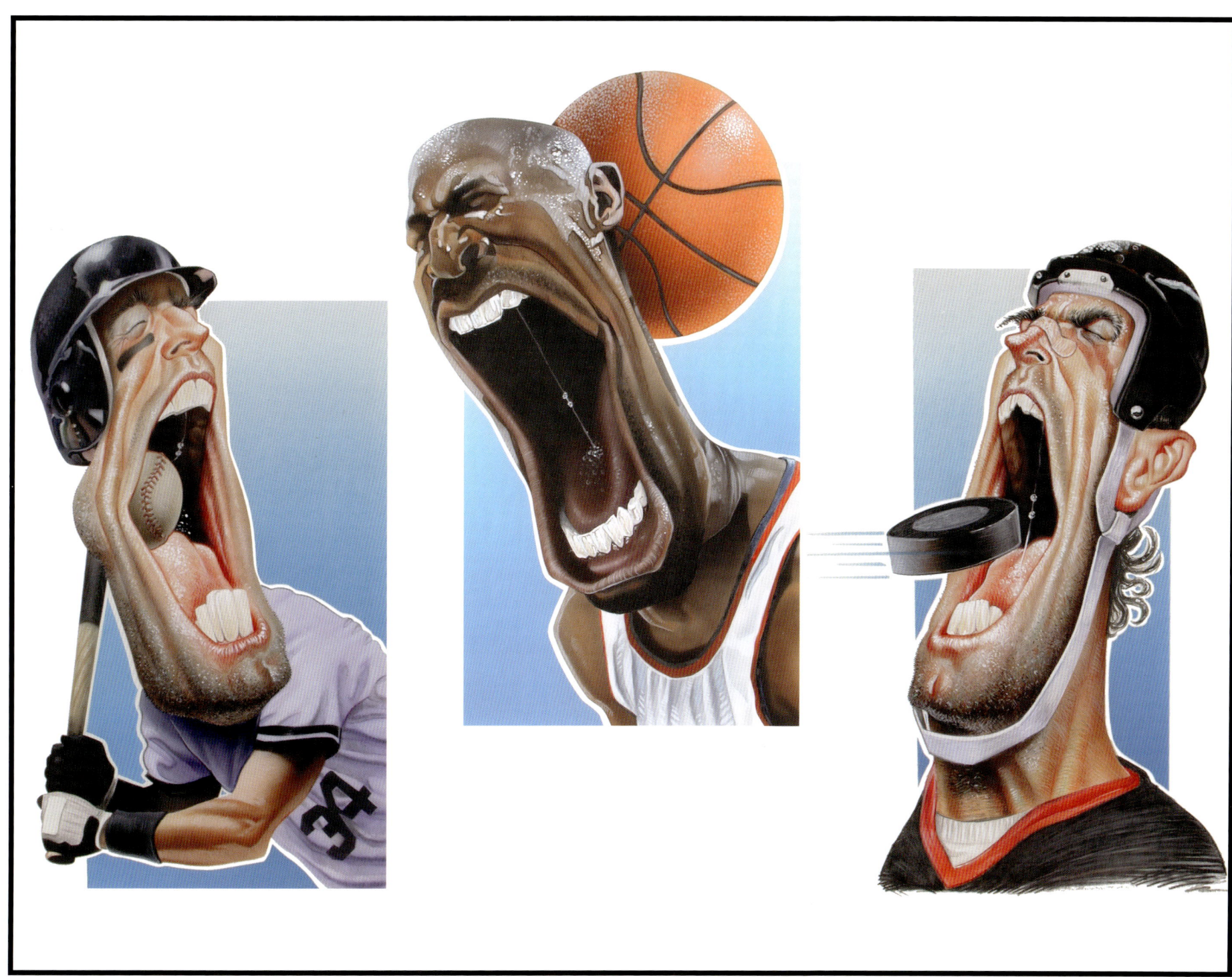

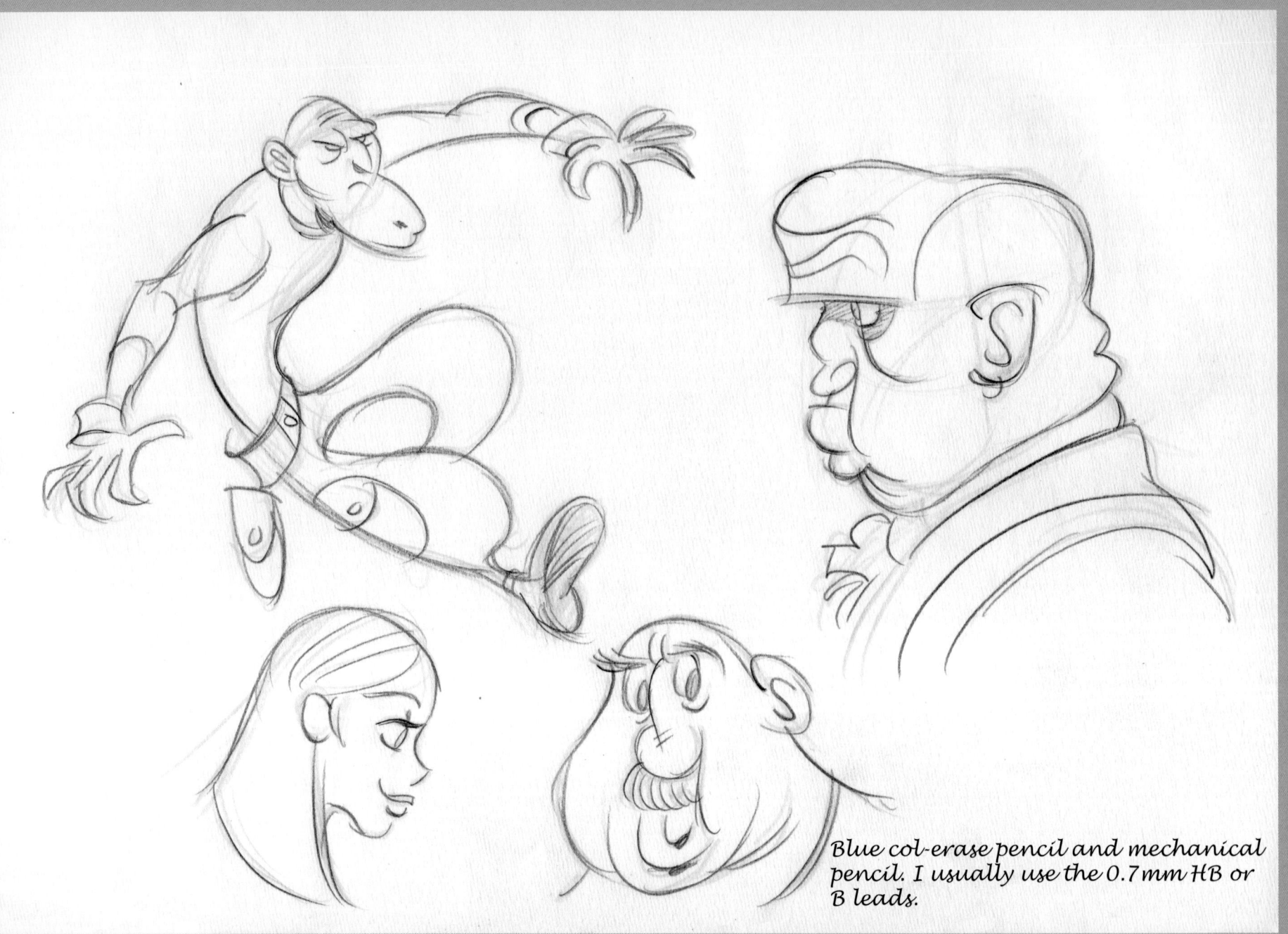

Blue col-erase pencil and mechanical pencil. I usually use the 0.7mm HB or B leads.

When I draw in my sketchbook I give myself one chance to get an image right. Some of the drawings have been thought through more and finished, while others that weren't working as well for me are left unfinished. For the last few years I have drawn in 9x12 sketchbooks. They are not too big and not too small, they are just right.

The looser I draw, the more freedom and fun I have. I am focusing on the overall shape and flow and not the details or cleanliness. It helps inspire new drawings and different approaches.

These heads were drawn from photographs with a blue pencil and Prismacolor pencil. I love Prismacolor pencils for the softness and boldness of the lead. They tend to glide so smoothly along the paper.

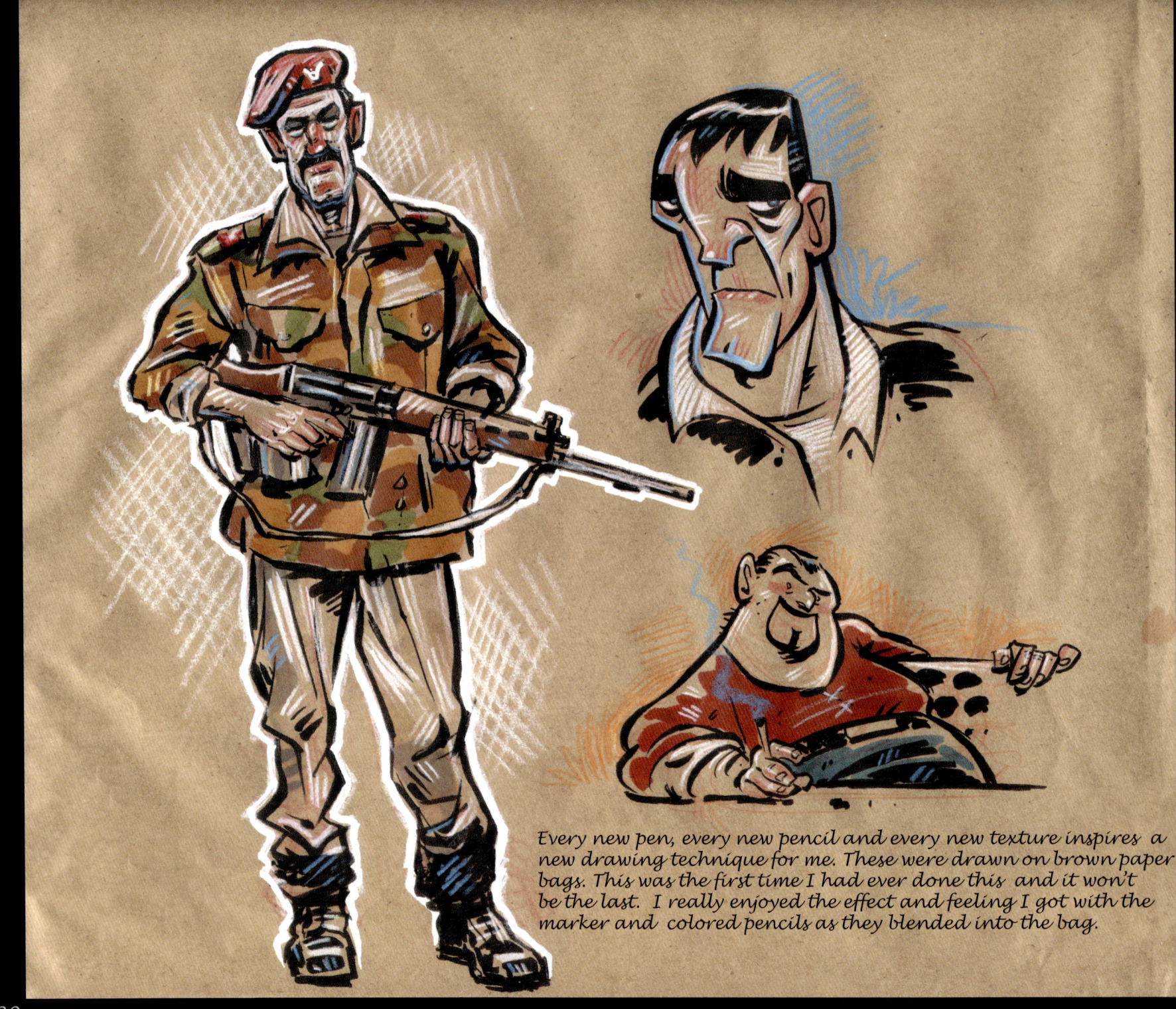

Every new pen, every new pencil and every new texture inspires a new drawing technique for me. These were drawn on brown paper bags. This was the first time I had ever done this and it won't be the last. I really enjoyed the effect and feeling I got with the marker and colored pencils as they blended into the bag.

Drawing in my sketchbook allows me to experiment. By keeping all my sketches loose, it gives me the opportunity to draw freely without doing to much thinking. Once I start tightening up my drawings I tend to lose a lot of the intended emotion.

When I was younger, I always wanted to have a style. "Style" to me was what being an artist was all about. I would get very frustrated that I didn't have one and felt that I would never become a real artist. As I got older, I began to feel that "style" could be somewhat restricting. By being committed to drawing eyes, noses, or clothes only one way, I wouldn't have given myself the opportunity to experiment as much as I did. So I have come to the conclusion that my "style" is to draw whatever I feel like drawing, anyway I want to with no restrictions. By not being so limited in style, I feel it gives me the flexibility of being able to adapt well in the animation industry. An industry which thrives on many different show styles and versatility. The more styles you know how to draw, the better chances you have of staying employed. The real goal is to learn the basic fundamentals of drawing and then just have fun.

This was the very first gouache painting I did back in 1999. The four drawings before the finish were the thumbnails to determine the lighting and the background.

Marker on vellum.

Gouache on board.

Gouache on board.

Pencil and ink wash on Bristol board.

This is an exercise I will do when I am trying to figure out different shapes for heads. At this stage it is more about the overall silhouette than the details within the face.

Above: Pencil and Prismacolor.

Marker on vellum.

Brush pen and marker.

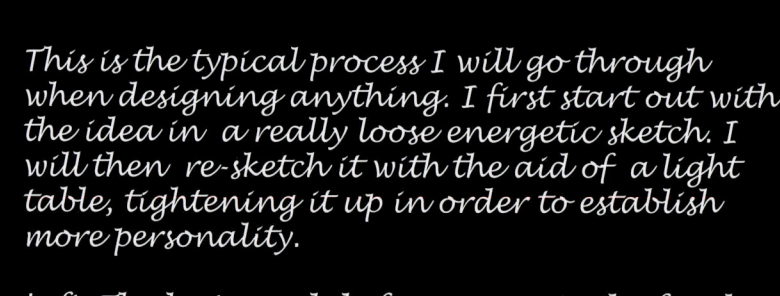

This is the typical process I will go through when designing anything. I first start out with the idea in a really loose energetic sketch. I will then re-sketch it with the aid of a light table, tightening it up in order to establish more personality.

Left: The last rough before going to the final as seen on the opposite page.

This was painted in watercolor, marker and Prismacolor.
It is based on an experience I endured on a plane flight.

My favorite art terms are rhythm and flow. It feels so natural and loose for me to draw this way. Every line seems to have its purpose as it flows into the next one.

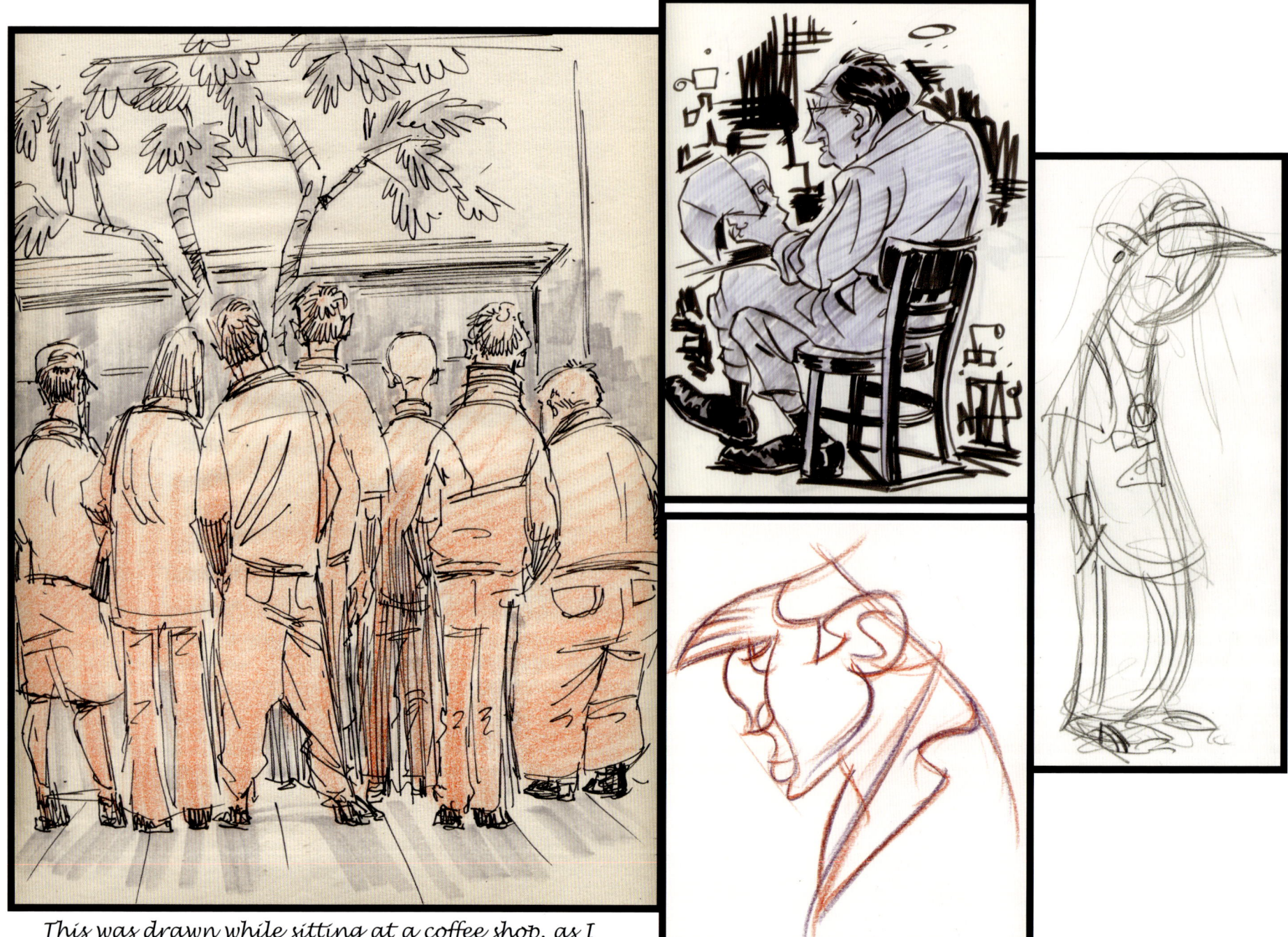

This was drawn while sitting at a coffee shop, as I watched a crowd observing a show on the Third Street Promenade in Santa Monica, CA.

Left: 25 second quick gesture studies in a coffee shop. Pen and marker on tracing paper.

Above: Quick sketches with brush pen at the airport. The faster I draw the better gesture I get.

Above: Ritmo B charcoal pencil on smooth newsprint.

Right: Prismacolor pencil on marker paper. Drawn from a live model.

I draw a lot of my designs really small on Post-it notes in order to establish basic shapes. I will then enlarge them on the copy machine, tighten them up and make any necessary changes I see fit.

Ink pen and wash on board.

Sepia brush pen.

Development sketches for a Nickelodeon pilot show called "Crash Nebula."

Above:
Five different versions of the same character I was developing for "Crash Nebula." I was simply exploring the different shapes that his body could have.

Right:
More develoment work for "Crash Nebula."

Early development sketches for the style of Nickelodeon's "Danny Phantom." I like to draw at least three characters on a page so that I can instantly see how they contrast each other in shape.

Pencil and watercolor.

75

I always like to exaggerate details as I did on this model drawn from life. Life drawing gives me the opportunity to experiment. I never just sit and copy the model, I am constantly improvising, mainly because I have never really studied the anatomy of a human and therefore rely on the basic shapes that are in front of me.

Drawn while watching Sumo wrestling on the television.

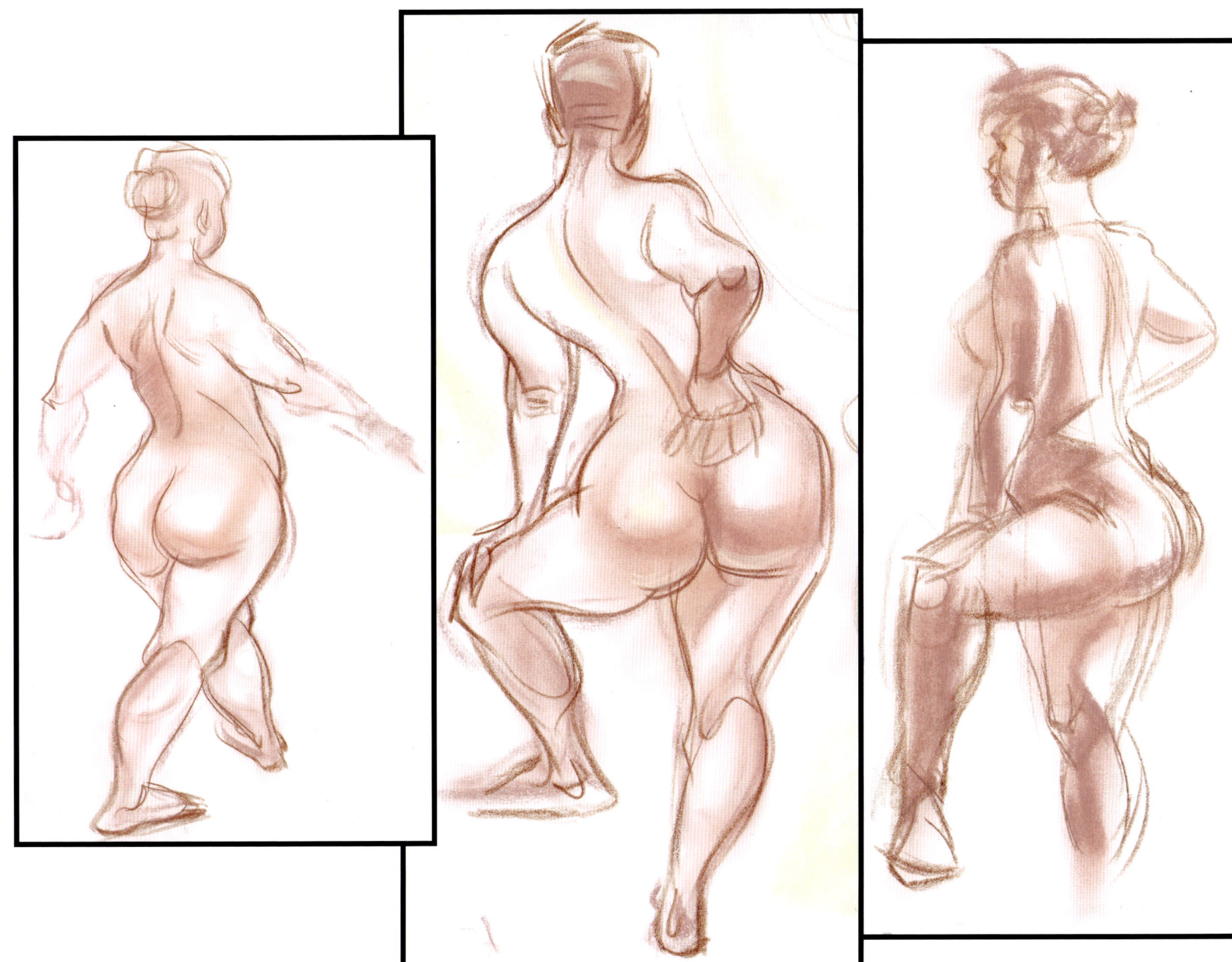

There are days when I go to draw and it flows. The drawing I want to do comes out of my hand the way I intended it to. Yet other times I feel like I don't know how to draw. These are the ups and downs I face as an artist. It is for this reason that I have to constantly practice drawing everyday.

Blue pencil underdrawing with grey markers.

The following paintings were inspired from the coffee shop. Believe it or not, I started the drawings by not looking at my paper and just sketching the heads from thoughts and feeling. I would then look at what I sketched, tighten them up and paint them with acrylics on canvas board. My journey as an artist constantly leads me through different phases of artistic expression.

Wildlife Force™ is an intellectual property that I created. This page is the front cover of my first comic book.

Opposite:
Pages of artwork featured in the comic book. They were drawn with black Prismacolor pencil and grey marker. In the middle of the following page is a maquette of my character, "Bamboo The Giant," sculpted by Tony Cipriano.

B.F. FERRET

KING KOMODO

ICE COLD PANTHERA

THE CROC

BAMBOO THE GIANT

THE POACHER

SLICKSTER

THE FLAME

THE QUAKE

The drawing above was the first rough I did on the piece to the right. I wasn't sure how I really wanted this pose to look until I went over it with a black Sharpie. By doing this it helped me make a confident choice to lift his leg up, thereby creating more of a dynamic gesture. The final was cleaned up with colored pencil and marker.

These were drawn on the same page to help with the shape variation of each character. Once again, I used the figure eight to help me in this process.

You will notice that the final marker drawings are mirror images of the roughs. By looking at the design in this way you will see all the flaws in it, mainly with the balance and construction. Therefore, I flip my drawings over and redraw them on the opposite side.

Above: Development sketch for Nickelodeon's "Danny Phantom."

SHAPE!
FORM!

119

These are concept roughs for the line of "Inaction Figures" based on Kevin Smith's movie "Dogma." If I ever need to make fixes on a design, I will use a Post-it note like I did here on the head of the character to the far right. It saves me from redrawing the whole image. It is the easiest and most efficient way to make changes on a design.

EYE

V SHAPE ON BOTTOM

This is the character Willam from the movie "Mallrats." It was the design for a T-shirt and the "Clerks Inaction Figure."

This was a T-shirt design drawn for Kevin Smith's company View Askew Productions and was featured at the 2003 Philadelphia Comic Convention. I typically draw lots of roughs and thumbnails to show Kevin; and when approved, I will ink it with a brush pen on animation paper.

Opposite:
Design for the 2003 Chicago Comic Convention.

Opposite below left:
Mr. Plug who was featured in the animated series and was one of the first designs I did for the show.

I did this design for View Askew's 2003 San Diego Comic Convention T-shirt.

Brush pen on animation paper.

Early development sketches for "Clerks: The Animated Series."

Right:
My first attempt on George Lucas. Quite often I will draw directly with a black Prismacolor pencil, it forces me to draw with a big bold confident line that I wouldn't achieve by using a thin blue pencil.

Development for "Danny Phantom."

Some of the very first development sketches for Nickelodeon's "Danny Phantom."

Development roughs for the Lunch Lady Character from "Danny Phantom." The two finished versions were cleaned up with a pen and colored in Photoshop.

From time to time I buy or make my own sketchbooks with colored paper. It is very helpful for me to change my canvas which in turn inspires me to draw in different ways. I love the way you can highlight with a white-out pen or colored pencil.

140

Coffee shop sketches. Pen and ink, colored pencil and marker on toned paper.

Finished turnaround and expressions for the dad in Nickelodeon's pilot episode "Crash Nebula."

Blue col-erase pencil sketches. Depending on my mood, I will usually do this as my under drawing before I lay ink or graphite on top.

At times I will sit in front of the TV and flip through channels looking for something interesting to draw. These were drawn while watching boxing. Often times I will tape a show and put it on pause which lasts a few minutes, this gives me enough time to capture a gesture.

149

Prismacolor pencil on animation paper.
Drawn from a black and white photo book on prisoners.

Coffee shop sketches. Pen and ink, colored pencil and white-out on toned paper. I don't focus so much on trying to get a likeness of the subject, but simply try to capture their character. I will often take a feature from one person and draw it on the next.

Prismacolor, marker and pencil.

I had one photograph from which I was trying to capture the likeness with. Usually I have at least 4-5 different views of the subject. As you can see I was playing with the proportions quite a bit until I decided to go with the sketches on the opposite page. I then transferred the image onto Bristol board and finished it up with airbrush and colored pencil.

Mouth wrong to much angle
Lower jaw wrong

Try putting mouth closer nose
Pull out jaw slightly

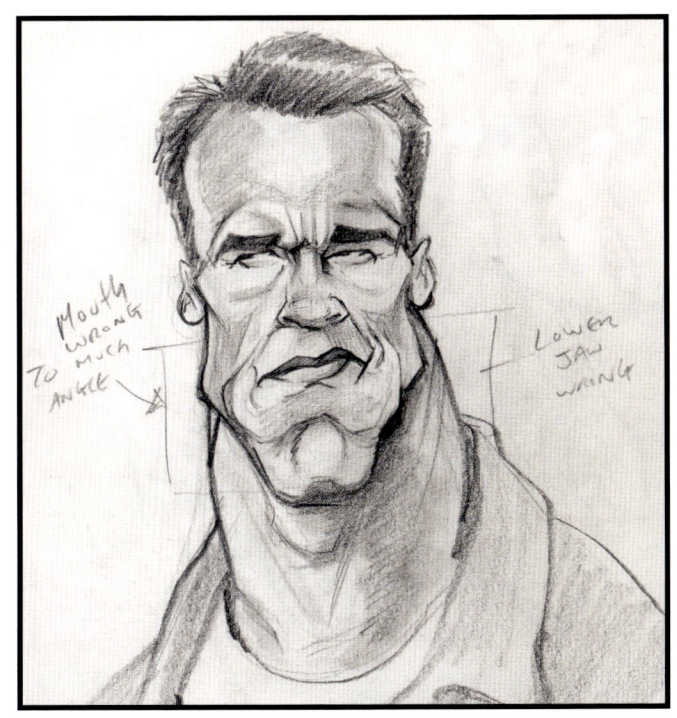

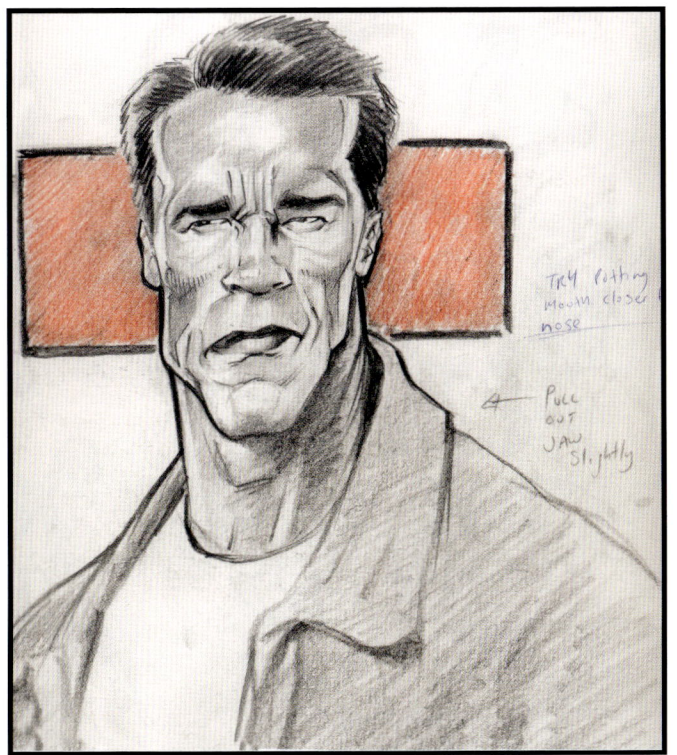

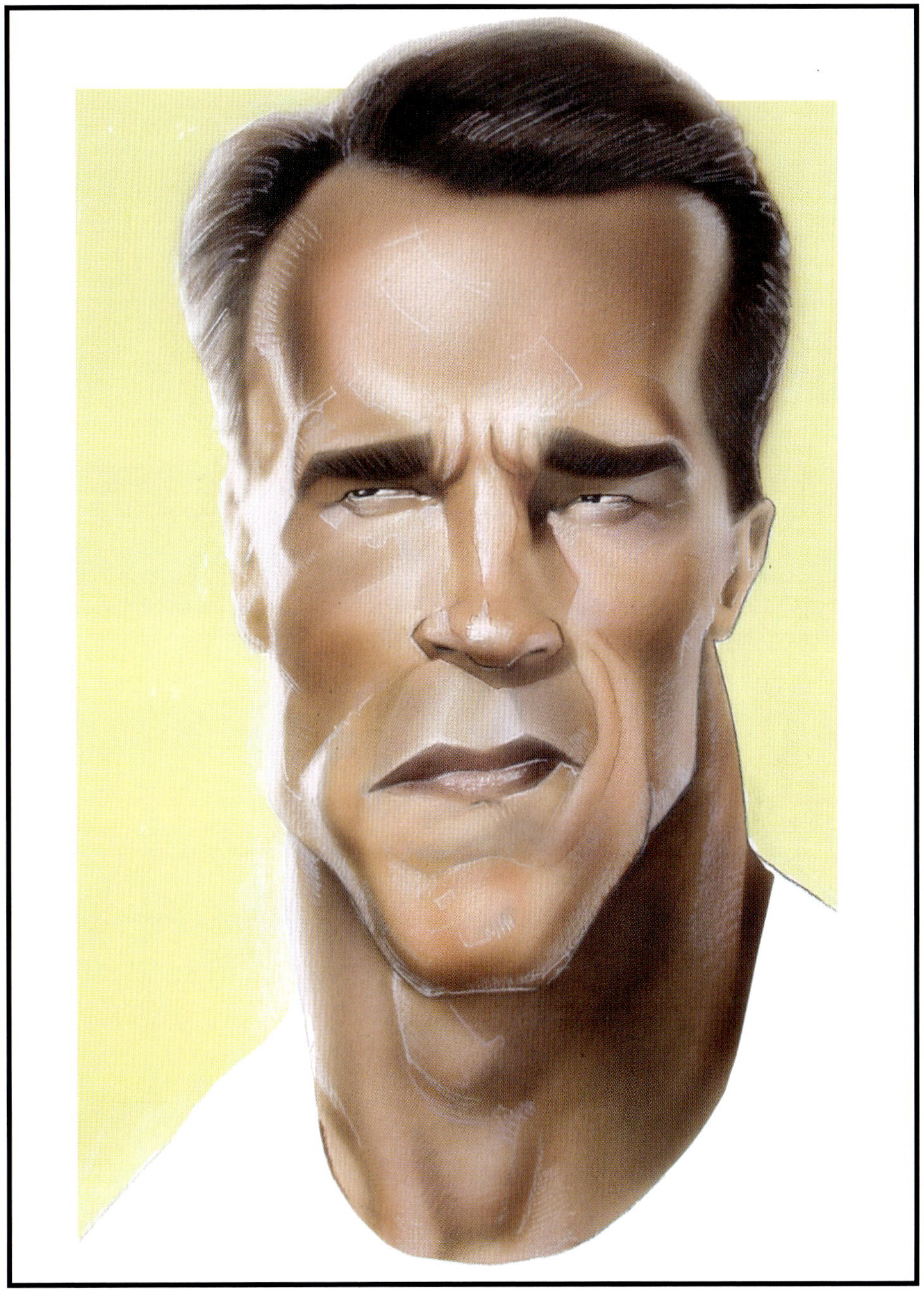

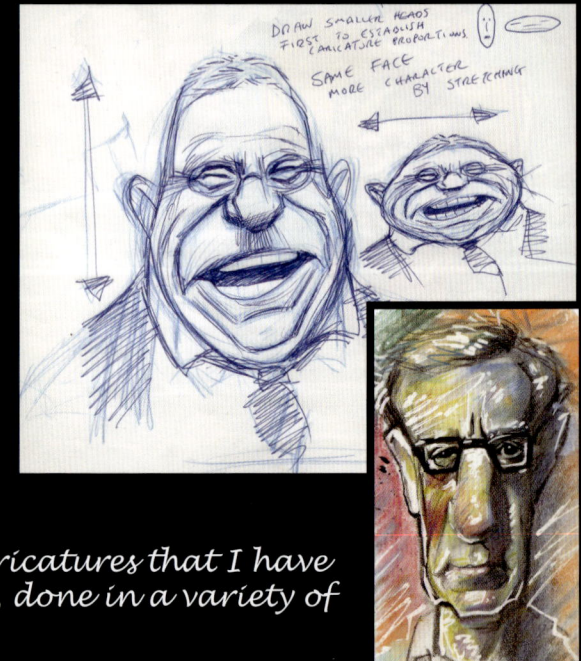

A small portion of caricatures that I have drawn over the years, done in a variety of mediums.

Backword

This is a story I like to tell when the occasion arises, for reasons I will elaborate on shortly:

In the 90's, while I was just getting started in the illustration/comic book business, I was spending a lot of time drawing live caricatures at my first theme park and retail caricature locations. During the Christmas season in 1992, I had a caricature booth at a mall in the northwestern Twin Cities suburb of Maplewood. I spent many a long weekday there, before the holiday crowds really arrived, working on drawings from photos and comic book pages, with an empty mall around me. On a particularly boring day I happened to notice, standing over my shoulder but a little way back, a funny looking kid with a big nose. He was watching me intently. I asked if he was waiting to get drawn, and he replied in an English accent that he was 'just watching'. I went about my drawing. He stayed and continued to watch. Hours went by, and this kid did not move. I kept glancing at him occasionally, and he was still watching intently. More hours went by, and still he stood quietly watching. I swear he never even went to the restroom. Finally I motioned to this kid to come over, and I asked him who he was, and what he was doing. His response was simply that he had heard about me from some caricaturists he worked with, and he was watching me to learn. It did not occur to him that standing still for hours and hours on end watching somebody draw was a nearly superhuman feat of concentration and endurance. This was my first meeting with Stephen Silver. He went on to work with me the next summer at my theme park operation at Valleyfair, and of course from there on to fame and fortune in the world of animation and cartooning. He also became a good friend.

The reason I like to tell that story is because it demonstrates some of the essential elements of Stephen that make him unique. You see, there are a lot of really talented artists out there in the world... people to whom life and all it's environments are a visual language they instinctively understand and can communicate fluently with and in.
There are also a lot of really hard working people out there in the world... people who focus on their goals and work tirelessly to achieve them, putting aside both ego and insecurity to recognize that they both have a lot to learn and the confidence that they can learn what they don't know. It's rare to find a combination of the immensely talented and the hard working, dedicated individual because the presence of one of these qualities often leads to (or results from) the absence of the other. When you have the rare individual who is intensely dedicated to the growth and improvement of their craft IN SPITE OF already being in possession of enormous talent... what you have there is someone special. Someone for whom the word 'potential' becomes an abstract, and limitless, boundary. Stephen Silver is one of those rare individuals. I'm excited to see where his art and his career take him...

Tom Richmond
(Mad Magazine Artist)

" Ya don't say, this is it, the end of the book."

**TO SEE MORE OF SILVER'S WORK
AND TO ORDER ADDITIONAL BOOKS
PLEASE VISIT**

WWW.SILVERTOONS.COM